# THE ROAD TO
# BERLIN

## Steven J. Zaloga and
## James Grandsen

ARMS AND
ARMOUR

**2.** During the course of the war the United States supplied the USSR with nearly 2,000 M4A2 (75mm) medium tanks. These began to be committed in heaviest numbers in the final years of the war, like this M4A2 knocked out in the Ukraine in the summer of 1944. (National Archives)

**3.** A column of Lend-Lease M4A2 medium tanks in a town in Byelorussia in the early summer of 1944. Operation 'Bagration' was the heaviest commitment of the Soviet mechanized forces in the war, including twelve tank and mechanized corps with some 5,200 tanks and self-propelled guns.

*Military Vehicles*

fotofax

# THE ROAD TO BERLIN

Steven J. Zaloga and
James Grandsen

**Front cover illustration:**
Panthers on the Eastern Front;
see illustration 16.

**Back cover:**
**Top:** An SU-76M in Prague, May
1945; see illustration 64.

**Bottom:** T-34-85s in Berlin; see
illustration 81.

**1.** It is often forgotten that the Wehrmacht on the Eastern Front was supported by allied Hungarian, Roumanian, and Finnish forces in the 1944 fighting. Here a Hungarian Turan tank and Csaba armoured car of the 2nd Armoured Division pass a German Panzerjaeger 38(t) 7.5cm tank destroyer during joint operations in Galicia in the Ukraine in the late spring/early summer of 1944. In 1944, the allied armies were a great worry to the Germans because of the possibility of their switching sides. However, Hungarian armoured units continued to serve with the Germans well into 1945, long after the Roumanians and Bulgarians had joined the Soviets. (Ivan Bajtos)

# INTRODUCTION

First published in Great Britain in 1990 by Arms and Armour Press, Artillery House, Artillery Row, London SW1P 1RT.

Distributed in the USA by Sterling Publishing Co. Inc., 387 Park Avenue South, New York, NY 10016-8810.

Distributed in Australia by Capricorn Link (Australia) Pty. Ltd, P.O. Box 665, Lane Cove, New South Wales 2066, Australia.

British Library Cataloguing in Publication Data
Zaloga, Steven J.
The road to Berlin. – (Military vehicles fotofax)
1. World War 2. Eastern European Campaigns
I. Title   II. Grandsen, James.
III. Series
940.54'21
ISBN 1-85409-014-3

Designed and edited by DAG Publications Ltd. Designed by David Gibbons; edited by David Gibbons; layout by Anthony A. Evans; typeset by Typesetters (Birmingham) Ltd and Ronset Typesetters Ltd; camerawork by M&E Reproductions, North Fambridge, Essex; printed and bound in Great Britain by The Alden Press Ltd, Oxford.

The aim of this book is to provide a photographic account of the final year of tank fighting on the Eastern Front, from the cataclysmic destruction of German Army Group Centre in Byelorussia in the summer of 1944 through to the final fighting around Berlin and Prague in May 1945. In preparing this book, the authors encountered the opposite problem faced in the earlier book *Operation 'Barbarossa'* (Tanks Illustrated No. 16). Photographic coverage of the 1944–5 fighting from the German perspective is quite limited, while Soviet coverage is much more extensive and available. Many of the German photos included here are from collections from friends in Eastern Europe who were able to locate German files left behind during the retreat of 1944–5, and they are seen here in print for the first time.

Tank battles of 1944–5 in Eastern Europe were the largest armoured clashes ever to occur – far larger in size and scope than such better known battles as the Kursk–Orel salient in 1943. Although these battles are well known to the Russians, they have been largely ignored by Western historians, who have been preoccupied with the great battles taking place in Western Europe at the time, especially the Normandy invasion and the battle for the Ardennes. The summer 1944 fighting on the Eastern Front started in earnest in June, in Byelorussia. By means of strategic deception, the Soviets bluffed the Germans into believing that the main thrust would come from the Ukrainian salient, aimed at Germany's wavering allies such as Roumania and Bulgaria. The Germans stripped their forces in Byelorussia in favour of units opposite the Ukraine. When the Soviet offensive hit Army Group Centre in June 1944, the Wehrmacht and Waffen SS had only about 550 tanks and assault guns in the area, only about 4 per cent of their holdings at the time. The Soviets massed 40 per cent of their tanks and assault guns, numbering 5,200 vehicles, opposite Army Group Centre. Army Group Centre was surrounded and smashed, with Soviet forces pouring into Poland and East Prussia. With the centre of the front penetrated, the Soviets launched attacks on the flanks as well, penetrating into Roumania and the western Ukraine in the late summer and clearing most of the eastern Baltic coast during the autumn fighting. By the early autumn, the force of the Soviet offensive was largely spent. Casualties had been very high, and supplies of fuel and ammunition had been exhausted.

During 1944, the Soviets manufactured nearly 29,000 new armoured vehicles yet lost nearly 25,000 due to battlefield attrition or mechanical exhaustion. Soviet armoured vehicle production in late 1944 shifted towards heavier vehicles such as the IS-2 heavy tank and its associated assault guns, the ISU-122 and ISU-152. This was largely in response to the German Panther tank, undoubtedly the finest German tank design of the war. In terms of technical quality, Soviet and German forces were more evenly matched than they had been earlier. While the Panther tank was superior to the much smaller T-34-85, a fairer comparison can be made between the Panther and the IS-2 Stalin heavy tank. German tank gun and tank ammunition technology was generally superior to Soviet guns of similar calibre, but the Soviets compensated for this by employing larger guns on smaller and lighter vehicles, thus redressing the balance.

Fighting continued all along the front during the autumn of 1944, but the Soviets conserved most of their new armoured forces for the final counter-offensive in January 1945. They carefully massed their new armoured forces, and built up large reserves of fuel and ammunition. The main thrust towards Berlin, called the Vistula–Oder offensive by the Soviets, involved over 7,000 Soviet tanks and assault guns opposed by about 1,200 German tanks and assault guns. By this stage in the war the Soviets had significant numerical advantages over the Germans, and the disparity in tactical skill between Soviet and German forces had narrowed. Although German tank units still enjoyed some advantages over their Soviet counterparts in terms of training and experience, this was not uniformly the case. Nor was the German advantage as great as in 1941–2. Some German units, such as the hastily raised Panther brigades, were not much better trained than their Soviet counterparts. The Germans also suffered from extreme supply problems, especially fuel supplies owing to the loss of the Roumanian oilfields in the autumn of 1944 and a vigorous Anglo-American and Soviet air bombing campaign. The supply problems severely limited the tactical mobility of German units in late 1944 and early 1945 and sapped their combat power.

By the time of the final drive on Berlin in April 1945, the outcome of the war was a foregone conclusion. The Vistula–Oder offensive had shattered most of the experienced German forces. The Soviet Army had over 214 divisions opposed by German units numbering 48 infantry, 6 tank and 8 motorized divisions. The Soviets massed 6,250 tanks and assault guns for the final operation, opposed by about 1,500 German tanks and self-propelled guns enfeebled by a lack of fuel or ammunition. The Soviets had a special advantage in artillery, with 41,600 guns and mortars and ample supplies of ammunition. The assault on Berlin took place in three stages, beginning on 16 April and lasting until the second week of May. Even after the surrender had taken place, tank fighting continued with isolated German units in Czechoslovakia until 11 May.

▼4

**4.** The Germans suffered massive losses of equipment during the Byelorussian summer offensive of 1944: here a 7.5cm Sturmgeschütz 40 Ausf G with the later style 'saukopf' gun mantlet and, in the background, a 10.5cm Sturmhaubitze 42. (Sovfoto)

**5 ▲**

**5.** The Germans were bluffed into believing that the main Soviet thrust in the summer of 1944 would be in the Ukraine, and so shifted their armour south. At the time of Operation 'Bagration', the Germans had only about 550 tanks and armoured vehicles with Army Group Centre, only 18 per cent of their armour on the Eastern Front, and only 4 per cent of their entire tank and self-propelled gun holdings. In contrast, the Soviets committed about 40 per cent of their tanks and self-propelled guns to the operation, overwhelming the Germans by factors of over 3-to-1. Here, a Pz Kpfw IV Ausf G lies knocked out in the summer 1944 fighting. From 30 June 1944 to 31 July 1944, the Wehrmacht lost 256 Pz Kpfw IV on the Eastern Front, mainly in Byelorussia. (Sovfoto)

**6.** By July, Soviet forces had crossed into Poland. Polish forces raised by the Soviet Union fought alongside Soviet troops. During the Vistula river campaign in Poland in August 1944, the Polish 1st Armoured Brigade was ferried across the river by ferry. Here a T-34 Model 43 of the 2nd Regiment drives onto the ramp with a Lend-Lease jeep lashed to its rear deck to conserve deck space.

**6 ▼**

**7.** During the fighting in the Studzianki bridgehead on the River Vistula, the Polish forces there had fifteen T-70 light tanks, which were used mainly for scouting and liaison. Armed with only a 45mm gun, the T-70 was of little use in tank fighting.

▲7

**8.** The Germans made vigorous efforts to smash the Soviet bridgeheads on the Vistula, especially at the Sandomierz bridgehead. here a disabled Pz Kpfw VI Ausf B Royal Tiger and a StuG III have been left behind on the battlefield, with a Soviet Maxim 7.62mm machine-gun in the foreground. The Germans lost at least five of these heavy tanks during the fighting there.

▲8  ▼9

**9.** The Hungarian Honved remained allied to Germany through the summer fighting. This Nimrod was one of seventeen serving with the 52nd Tank Destroyer Battalion of 2nd Hungarian Armoured Division in Galicia, south-eastern Poland, in the summer of 1944. The Nimrod was a licence-built derivative of a Swedish Landsverk design. By this stage of the war, its 40mm gun was hopelessly inadequate against Soviet armour. (Ivan Bajtos)

**10.** One of the odder armoured vehicles to see service on the Eastern Front was the German Ladungstraeger B IV, a remotely controlled engineer vehicle used to carry and deposit large breeching charges against heavily protected enemy fortifications. These were used in significant numbers during the August 1944 Warsaw Uprising, where they were used to blast away street barricades erected by the Polish insurgents. They were usually controlled by special radio-equipped StuG III assault guns.

**11.** A rather strange tank to find in Poland in 1944 – this ex-Italian M14/41 was being used by a German anti-partisan unit in the Warsaw area when captured by the Polish Home Army during the Warsaw Uprising in August 1944.

10▲    11▼

**12.** The Polish Home Army captured several German armoured vehicles during the uprising, including at least two Panther tanks. They were attached to the armoured platoon of the 'Radoslaw' group and took part in the fighting during the second week of August. The Poles also captured and used a Hetzer and an Sd Kfz 251 Ausf D; the latter is currently preserved at the Polished Armed Forces Museum in Warsaw.

**13.** In late July 1944, the 1st Ukrainian Front seized the city of Lwow. Here, being examined by civilians is a disabled Panther Ausf A, one of some 219 Panthers lost on the Eastern Front in July 1944. (Sovfoto)

▲12    ▼13

**14.** The PT-34 mine-clearing vehicle consisted of the T-34 tank (in this case a Model 43) and a Mugalev mine roller. These were employed by special engineer tank regiments with 22 T-34 tanks and 18 mine trawls each. About five of these regiments were in service in 1944/5 for minefield breaching operations.

14▲

**15.** A Panther Ausf A tank knocked out during fighting in the summer of 1944. A single hit can be seen at the lip of the hull superstructure and a glancing shot off the upper left edge of the gun mantlet.

15▲    16▼

**16.** A unit of Panther Ausf A tanks in operations on the Eastern Front in the summer of 1944. By this time, the Panther was the most numerous German tank, slightly outnumbering the older and less effective Pz Kpfw IV.

**17.** A Panther Ausf A in action in Poland in the late summer of 1944. At this stage of the war the Panther outclassed the smaller and lighter T-34-85 but was more evenly matched against the IS-2 tank. Although the Germans classified the Panther as a medium tank and the Soviets classed the IS-2 as a heavy tank, they were comparable in both weight and size.

▲17

**18.** A Hungarian Turan tank of the 2nd Hungarian Armoured Division in eastern Poland, summer 1944. By this stage of the war, the Turan's 40mm gun was inadequate for tank fighting, but newer designs were not yet ready. In front of the Turan is a German Pz Kpfw IV. (Ivan Bajtos)

▲18    ▼19

**19.** Armour encountered by Soviet forces in Hungary included Hungarian assault guns like this Zrinyi II assault gun armed with a 105mm howitzer. The Turan IIs saw combat action in Galicia, eastern Poland, from the spring of 1944 and later in the fierce fighting in Hungary and Czechoslovakia. This particular Zrinyi II, named Renke, is fitted with skirt armour and spare track to supplement its inadequate protection. This particular vehicle was captured by the Soviets and is currently preserved at the Kubinka proving grounds outside Moscow.

**20.** Hungarian armoured forces were dependent on domestic production for the majority of their equipment. The Turan III seen here in prototype form was an attempt to uparm the Turan with a long 75mm tank gun to give it the capability of dealing with the Soviet T-34. It was never series-produced, and Hungarian units were forced to rely on more poorly armed versions. (Ivan Bajtos)

20▲

**21.** On 20 August 1944, the 2nd and 3rd Ukrainian Fronts crashed into Roumania, spearheaded by 1,890 tanks and assault guns. Called the Jassy-Kishniev offensive, the Soviet forces faced 404 German and Roumanian tanks and assault guns. Here a Soviet SU-85 tank destroyer enters Bacau, near Bucharest, on 31 August 1944, six days after Roumania switched sides. The SU-85 was the first major Soviet self-propelled gun specifically designed as a tank destroyer. By the end of 1944 it was gradually being supplanted by the more powerful SU-100.

21▲    22▼

**22.** During fighting in Poland in October 1944, this Panther Ausf A and Jagdpanzer IV tank destroyer were put out of action when they accidently collided. A total of 55 Jagdpanzer IVs were lost on the Eastern Front in October 1944, and 381 Panthers.

▲23 ▼24

**23.** A pair SU-152 assault guns of the 2nd Baltic Front wade across a river in Latvia in August 1944 during the assaults against Army Group North. The Baltic fighting was given less priority by the Soviets than the drives into Poland and Roumania but became the scene of bitter fighting as the Soviets first crossed into German soil in East Prussia during the autumn of 1944. (Sovfoto)

**24.** A Soviet Valentine Mk VIII scout tank of the 3rd Byelorussian Front crosses Cathedral Square in Vilno. Britain and Canada provided the Soviets with 3,782 of these tanks. By 1944, they were nearly worthless for tank fighting, but the Soviets found them very useful for scouting and other tasks. (Sovfoto)

25▲

26▲    27▼

**25.** A column of Panther Ausf G tanks operating in the autumn/winter of 1944, probably in East Prussia. These vehicles are finished in a type of speckle camouflage seen only during the final months of the war.

**26.** An IS-2 heavy tank of the 2nd Baltic Front passes through a wood to the east of Riga in September 1944. The IS-2 tank was first extensively used in combat in the summer fighting of 1944. It was the most powerful Soviet tank of the war and the only Soviet tank that could seriously challenge the highly effective Panther. (Sovfoto)

**27.** A Panther Ausf G tank in Latvia during the fighting in 1944. At this time, Army Group North had about 110 Panthers out of the 730 tanks and assault guns operating there.

▲28   ▼29

**28.** A Tiger I tank carries German airborne troops into action somewhere in East Prussia in the autumn of 1944. There were about 80 Tiger I and Tiger II tanks with Army Group North at the time, mainly with Heavy Tank Battalion 502.

**29.** A knocked out T-34-85 is examined by German infantry in East Prussia during the autumn of 1944. Although Soviet forces crossed the German frontier during the 1944 fighting, there was a relative lull in the Baltic region in December 1944 as the Soviets prepared for their massive January 1945 offensive.

**30.** A T-34-85 tank captured by German forces in East Prussia in the autumn of 1944 and impressed into their service. The use of the T-34-85 by German forces was uncommon, as few were captured intact at this stage of the war.

**31.** German troops examine a thoroughly destroyed ISU-152 assault gun during the autumn of 1944. The vehicle presumably suffered an internal explosion, which ripped off the right side of the superstructure and roof.

**32.** A Panther Ausf G seeks out targets somewhere in Hungary in the autumn of 1944. To the right is a Sd Kfz 250/8 75mm light assault gun, used mainly in light armoured scout companies.

30▲

31▲     32▼

▲33

▲34 ▼35

**33.** A pair of 15cm Panzerwerfer 42 auf Sf abandoned during the fighting in the winter of 1944. These multiple rocket launchers have apparently been bogged down in a swamp.

**34.** A T-34 Model 43 in East Prussia in the winter of 1944/5. Although out of production by the end of 1944, the older models of the T-34 still appeared in action until eventually lost through attrition.

**35.** A Panther tank being used to transport German infantry, somewhere on the Eastern Front, in the winter of 1944/5. German armoured units reached their peak strength in the East in November 1944 but gradually lost strength as vehicles were transferred west for the Ardennes offensive in December 1944.

**36.** This Panther was one of 32 tanks and assault guns knocked out during the fighting for Poznan in January-February 1945. From the two large penetrations in the hull front, it seems likely that it was a victim of one of the IS-2 tanks used by the 1st Guards Tank Army in the battle. (Sovfoto)

**37.** A Sd Kfz 251/21 anti-aircraft vehicle abandoned by German troops in the battle for Festung Breslau (currently Wroclaw, Poland), one of 40 armoured vehicles lost by German forces there. The fighting for the city was savage, and the German garrison did not finally surrender until 6 May 1945. (Sovfoto)

▲38  ▼39

**38.** A Polish T-34-85 of the 1st Armoured Brigade reaches the Baltic in February 1945, and the tank symbolically dips its tracks in the sea as one of its crew displays the national flag. This unit took part in the liberation of Gdansk and Gdynia.

**39.** A Tiger I heavy tank knocked out during fighting in Poland, with a knocked out Tiger II behind it. The Tiger I and Tiger II were both respected by their Soviet opponents, and constituted a major reason for the Soviet shift in 1944 to the production of more heavily armed vehicles such as the IS-2, ISU-122 and SU-100.

**40.** The shattered carcass of a Soviet IS-2m heavy tank forms the basis for an improvised road sign on the outskirt of a Polish town in 1945.

**41.** An IS-2m heavy tank of an independent heavy tank regiment on the 3rd Byelorussian Front overruns a barbed wire obstacle during the fighting in East Prussia in January 1945. The winter offensive began on 13 January and employed four tank and one mechanized corps with a total of 3,859 tanks and assault guns. German forces in the area totalled about 940 tanks and assault guns.

**42.** A German armoured column destroyed by forces of the Soviet 2nd Byelorussian Front in February 1945. The assault guns are StuG IV, a less common version of assault gun than the StuG III. Of the 940 German tanks and assault guns with Army Group North during the East Prussian campaign, about 60 per cent were assault guns, mainly StuG III and StuG IV. (Sovfoto)

40▲

41▲　　42▼

▲43  ▼44                                                    ▲45

**43.** An ISU-152 assault gun crew takes a breather during the January 1945 offensive. This assault gun, based on the chassis of the IS-2 Stalin heavy tank, proved to be a popular vehicle during street fighting in 1945 because of its heavy armour and the heavy high-explosive shell it could fire.

**44.** Soviet troops advance through the streets of Tolkemit on the Baltic in the spring of 1945. They pass the charred wreck of a Pz Kpfw 38(t). This old tank is an odd vehicle to see still in action in 1945, and it was probably attached to an anti-partisan unit or school rather than to a regular tank unit. (Sovfoto)

**45.** A battery of SU-76m assault guns of Konev's 1st Ukrainian Front move through the town of Neisse following the Vistula–Oder offensive of January–February 1945. The SU-76 was the second most common armoured vehicle in Soviet service in 1945, and was exceeded in numbers only by the T-34 tank. It was most commonly used to provide direct-fire support to infantry units. (Sovfoto)

**46.** SU-100s enter the town of Landsberg during the spring 1945 fighting. The SU-100 first saw extensive fighting in the January–February offensives. It was intended as a medium tank destroyer, and was probably the most effective vehicle of its type developed by the Soviets during the war. (Sovfoto)

**47.** Roumania switched sides in 1944 and supported Soviet operations in 1945 in Czechoslovakia. One of the odder armoured vehicles in service was the TACAM T-60. This was an improvised tank destroyer built in Roumania using captured Soviet T-60 light tank hulls and captured 76.2mm F-22 divisional guns. The Roumanians also used the R-2 TACAM, which consisted of the imported Czechoslovak R-2, better known as the Pz Kpfw 35(t), and captured Soviet 76.2mm ZiS divisional guns. These unusual Eastern Front vehicles are shown in the accompanying scale plans in this book.

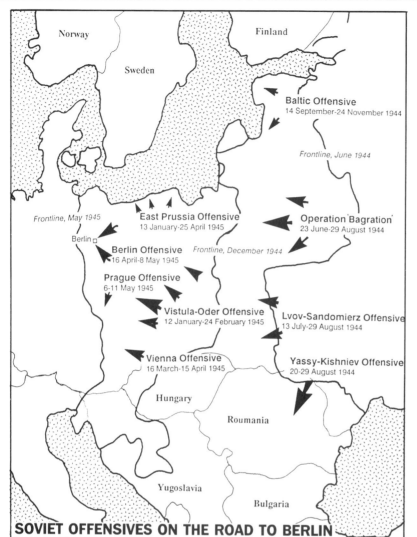

## SOVIET OFFENSIVES ON THE ROAD TO BERLIN

Map labels:
- Norway
- Finland
- Sweden
- Baltic Offensive 14 September-24 November 1944
- Frontline, June 1944
- Frontline, May 1945
- Berlin
- East Prussia Offensive 13 January-25 April 1945
- Operation Bagration 23 June-29 August 1944
- Berlin Offensive 16 April-8 May 1945
- Frontline, December 1944
- Prague Offensive 6-11 May 1945
- Vistula-Oder Offensive 12 January-24 February 1945
- Lvov-Sandomierz Offensive 13 July-29 August 1944
- Vienna Offensive 16 March-15 April 1945
- Yassy-Kishniev Offensive 20-29 August 1944
- Hungary
- Roumania
- Yugoslavia
- Bulgaria

## SOVIET T-34-85 TANK INTERIORS

Hull front ▶

1. Seat for co-driver
2. Stowage racks for DT machine-gun ammunition
3. Belly escape hatch
4. Clutch
5. Gear-box
6. Manual fuel lever
7. Accelerator pedal
8. Brake pedal
9. Safety catch for brake pedals
10. Driver's seat
11. Left brake pedal
12. Fire extinguisher
13. Air pressure valve for engine starter
14. Lubricant pump
15. Housing for suspension spring
16. Air pressure switch
17. Electrical panel
18. Air pressure adjustment (for engine starting)
19. RRA-24F regulator
20. Hydraulic cylinder for front hatch
21. Intercom button
22. Tachometer
23. Speedometer
24. Brake lever
25. Front hatch opening
26. Hand operated air pump
27. Air bottles for engine starting
28. Driving control dials
29. Intercom control box
30. Machine-gun lock
31. DTM machine-gun stock
32. DTM machine-gun ball mount
33. Interior light socket
34. Main switch
35. Main gun ammunition stowage

## TECHNICAL COMPARISON OF THE GERMAN AND SOVIET TANKS OF 1944–5

| | Pz Kpfw IV Ausf J | T-34-85 Model 1944 | Panther Ausf G | IS-2m | | Pz Kpfw IV Ausf J | T-34-85 Model 1944 | Panther Ausf G | IS-2m |
|---|---|---|---|---|---|---|---|---|---|
| Weight (tonnes) | 25 | 32 | 46 | 46 | Engine horsepower | 300 | 500 | 700 | 600 |
| Crew | 5 | 5 | 5 | 4 | HP/Weight ratio | 1:12 | 1:15.6 | 1:15.2 | 1:13 |
| Length (cm) | 702 | 815 | 886 | 990 | Maximum road speed (km/h) | 38 | 55 | 46 | 37 |
| Width (cm) | 288 | 300 | 340 | 309 | Maximum range (km) | 320 | 360 | 200 | 240 |
| Height (cm) | 268 | 260 | 298 | 273 | Turret front armour (mm) | 50 | 90 | 110 | 160 |
| Main gun calibre (mm) | 75 | 85 | 75 | 122 | Turret side armour (mm) | 30 | 75 | 45 | 110 |
| Gun length in calibres | 48 | 55 | 70 | 46 | Turret rear armour (mm) | 30 | 60 | 45 | 100 |
| Armour Piercing (kg) | 6.8 | 9.02 | 6.8 | 48.7 | Hull glacis armour (mm) | 80 | 47 | 80 | 120 |
| APHE penetration at 500m (mm) | 105 | 111 | 135 | 145 | Hull side armour (mm) | 30 | 60 | 50 | 95 |
| APHE penetration at 1000m (mm) | 95 | 102 | 120 | 145 | Hull rear armour (mm) | 20 | 47 | 45 | 30 |
| Armour Piercing (DS) (kg) | 4.1 | 4.9 | 4.75 | — | | | | | |
| APDS penetration at 500m (mm) | 130 | 138 | 190 | — | | | | | |
| APDS penetration at 1000m (mm) | 105 | 100 | 160 | — | | | | | |

# SOVIET T-34-85 HULL FRONT INTERIOR

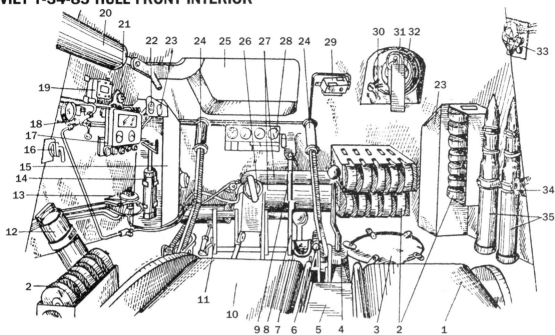

## Turret Interior ▼

1. Loader's seat
2. Gunner's seat
3. Turret traverse
4. Turret race
5. Pistol port
6. Turret illumination switch
7. Junction box
8. Periscope
9. TSh-16 telescope sight
10. Sight illumination switch
11. 85mm main gun
12. Ventilator
13. Turret lamp
14. DTM co-axial machine-gun
15. DTM ammunition drum racks
16. Turret race lock

# SOVIET T-34-85 TURRET FRONT

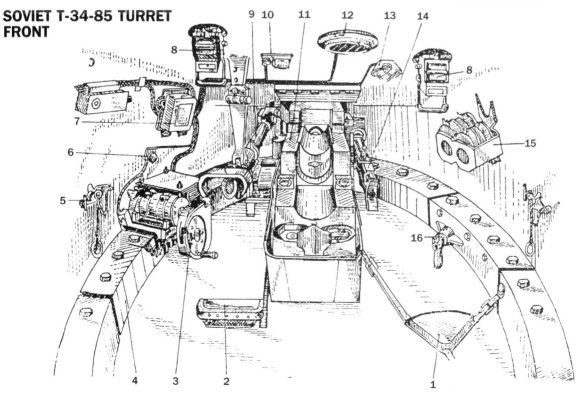

# IS-2m

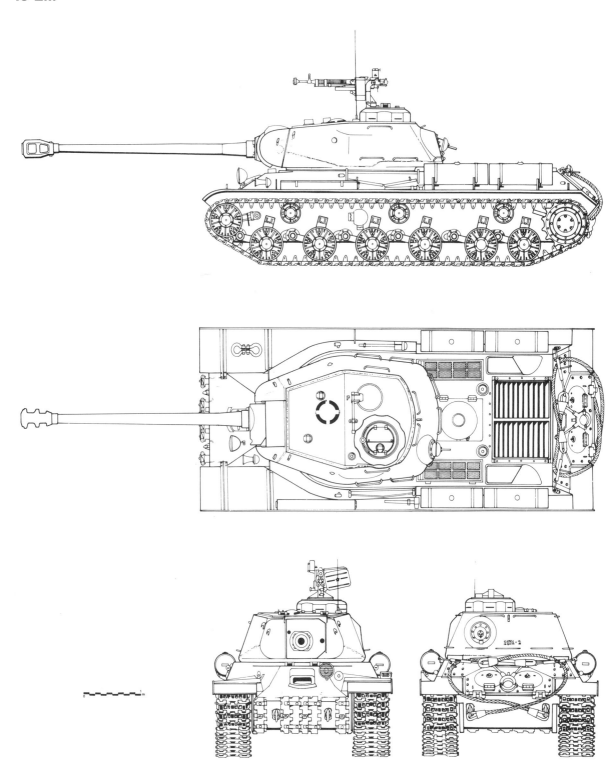

# TACAM (R-2)

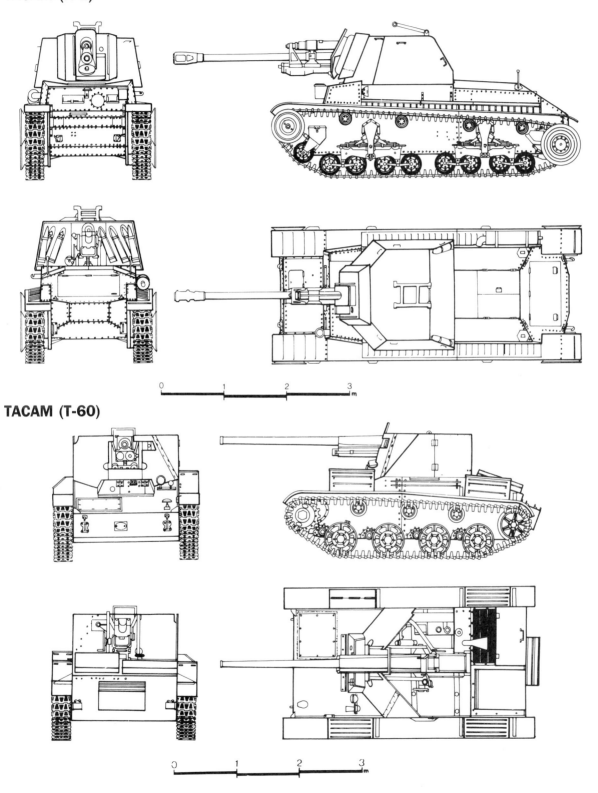

# TACAM (T-60)

▲ 48

▲ 49    ▼ 50

**48.** A column of T-34-85 tanks of Konev's 1st Ukrainian Front in Tost, Silesia, in February 1945. The 1st Ukrainian Front's drive placed them opposite Breslau by 3 February 1945. The Vistula–Oder offensive was the largest single element of the Soviet thrust in January 1945, involving about 7,000 Soviet tanks and assault guns against about 1,220 German tanks and assault guns. (Sovfoto)

**49.** A BA-64B armoured scout car of the 2nd Byelorussian Front stands guard in the town square of Stulp in March 1945. The BA-64 was based on the chassis of the GAZ-67 jeep and was the only wheeled armoured vehicle produced in any significant numbers by the Soviets during the war. (Sovfoto)

**50.** Although not of the best quality, this rare photo shows one of the least known combatants of the 1944–5 fighting, a Pz Kpfw IV tank of the Bulgarian Armoured Brigade, during operations near Dravasza-Bolcs in Hungary in 1944. The Bulgarians had been partially equipped by the Germans up to the summer of 1944, but in September 1944 they switched sides and fought against the Wehrmacht, mainly in Yugoslavia. (Ivan Bajtos)

**51.** A Polish SU-85 of the 13th Assault Gun Regiment during the fighting in 1945. On the wall is the slogan 'Polish Soldiers Are Going to Berlin'. The vehicle number '330' evident on the glacis plate identifies it as the command vehicle of the 3rd battery.

**52.** A BA-64B armoured car with civilians on board precedes a T-34-85 down a road in the Slovakian countryside. The BA-64 was commonly used as a command and liaison vehicle in Soviet armoured units. (Ivan Bajtos)

**53.** Soviet troops paint a slogan which appears to say 'Death to Goebbels' on the side of a captured Hanomag Sd Kfz 251/17 anti-aircraft halftrack.

**54.** The Polish LWP armoured units were provided with a number of Lend-Lease Universal carriers, this particular one serving with the 2nd Polish Army, probably with the 20th Motorcycle Battalion. The troops are armed with an assortment of Soviet small arms, including a PTRS anti-tank rifle and a DP light machine-gun.

**55.** A Soviet armoured column of 9th Guards Tank Brigade, 1st Guards Mechanized Corps, in Vienna in the spring of 1945. Their vehicles are Lend-Lease M4A2 (76mm) medium tanks.

▲53　▼54

The entire 1st Mechanized Corps was equipped with American Lend-Lease tanks.

**56.** A repair yard in Vienna following the fighting there in April 1945 consists of a strange collection of tanks including German Panthers, ex-French Renault FT light tanks, and ex-Italian M.14/41 tanks. These captured types were probably being used in the area for security deals.

**57.** A Lend-Lease M3A1 scout car is used by Soviet reconnaissance units during the fighting in Vienna in March–April 1945. Aside from modest numbers of BA-64B scout cars, the Soviets mainly used Lend-Lease M3A1 scout cars or Universal carriers in their mechanized scout units. (Sovfoto)

55▲

56▲    57▼

▲58   ▼59

**58.** A Soviet tank crew poses with members of a Czechoslovak resistance group on 9 May 1945. The tank is a Lend-Lease M4A2 medium tank, widely used in the final months of the war. (Ivan Bajtos)

**59.** A Ya-12 artillery tractor towing a BS-3 100mm Model 1944 anti-tank gun near Jihlava, Czechoslovakia, on 9 May 1945. The Ya-12 tractor was derived from the T-60/T-70 light tank series and was used for towing larger artillery pieces, especially anti-tank and anti-aircraft guns. (Ivan Bajtos)

**60.** A Hetzer tank destroyer in operation in Czechoslovakia on the last day of fighting, 9 May 1945. These small tank destroyers were relatively prevalent in the fighting in Czechoslovakia in May 1945 for the obvious reason that they were manufactured there. (Ivan Bajtos)

60▲

**61.** A Hetzer tank destroyer carries an infantry section during fighting in Czechoslovakia on 9 May 1945. (Ivan Bajtos)

61▲     62▼

**62.** During the fighting on 9 May 1945, several Hetzers were knocked out by Soviet Forces. The Hetzer was very thinly armoured and no match for most tanks of the period except from ambush. (Ivan Bajtos)

▲63  ▼64

65▲

**63.** An SU-76M in Prague in the first week of May 1945. The Prague operation involved the 1st, 2nd and 4th Ukrainian Fronts, and 1960 tanks and self-propelled guns. German mechanized forces in the area were quite strong, nearly equal to Soviet forces, but were not very effective as many units were fleeing westward to avoid capture by the Soviets. (CTK via Jir Hornat)

**64.** A column of SU-100 tank destroyers ambushed near Brno, Czechoslovakia, in April 1945. The vehicles lack their wheels, which suggests that the local peasant carts may have benefitted! As late as the 1970s it was possible to see small carts in Poland and Czechoslovakia with wheels taken from various derelict Soviet and German armoured vehicles in 1945. (Ivan Bajtos)

**65.** A German 15cm SIG 33/1 Grille on the streets of Prague in May 1945 preparing to meet the Soviet onslaught. There was a significant amount of fighting in the streets of Prague between the Germans, Czech insurgents and Soviet troops. (Ivan Bajtos)

**66.** A column of T-34-85 tanks of the Polish 16th Armoured Brigade in Prague in May 1945. Polish troops fought alongside Soviet and Czechoslovak units during the final phases of the Czechoslovakia fighting.

66▼

**67.** A German Sd Kfz 250 halftrack captured by Czech insurgents in Prague during the May 1945 uprising. Captured armour was usually painted with a prominent CSR, meaning Czechoslovak Republic. (CTK via Jiri Hornat)

**68.** In the shadows of the Royal Palace, a German Hetzer tank destroyer ambushed a T-34-85 of the 63rd Guards Tank Brigade, 10th Guards Tank Corps, numbered '24' and commanded by Lieutenant Goncharenko. The Hetzer was then knocked out by other T-34-85s, which were following. This event is commemorated by a tank monument in Prague – but ironically the monument consists of an IS-2 numbered '23', even though it is supposed to represent Goncharenko's tank. (CTK via Jir Hornat)

**69.** A Soviet IS-2m heavy tank enters the town of Hradec Kralove in north-eastern Bohemia in May 1945. Independent heavy tank regiments using the IS-2 were frequently employed as spearheads for Soviet armoured attacks during the last months of the war because of their superior armour protection and firepower. (CTK via Jiri Hornat)

**70.** A T-34-85 enters the town of Budyne in north-western Bohemia in May 1945. By this phase of the war, the German resistance was largely collapsing as units tried to flee westward. However, there were several sharp tank encounters, even after the surrender had been signed. (CTK via Jiri Hornat)

**71.** A number of Bergepanzer 38(t) Hetzer recovery vehicles took part in the fighting in Prague in May 1945, and at least one fell into the hands of Czech insurgents. (Ivan Bajtos)

**72.** A column of T-34-85s of the 1st Czechoslovak Independent Tank Brigade enter the Old Town Square in Prague, May 1945. This was the only Czechoslovak large tank unit formed under Soviet tutelage during the war. (CTK via Jiri Hornat)

**73.** A heavily decorated Hetzer tank destroyer in the hands of Czech insurgents in Prague in May 1945. The Hetzer was manufactured at the CKD facility in the outskirts of Prague, and many of the Hetzers used by the insurgents were vehicles found at the factory without their gun. The slogans painted on the side say 'Death to the Occupiers'. (CTK via Jiri Hornat)

◀71    ▼72

73▲

▲74　▼75

**74.** Soviet mobile air defence units received 1,000 of these Lend-Lease M17 multiple gun motor carriages from the United States during the war, this particular example seeing service in Prague in 1945. (Ivan Bajtos)

**75.** An SU-57 tank destroyer, better known by its American designation, the T48 57mm tank destroyer, in Prague in May 1945. The T48 was developed at British request, but saw combat service only with Soviet units, to whom some 650 were supplied. (CTK via Jiri Hornat)

**76.** A T-34-85 in Germany, May 1945, named in honour of Vladimir Moyakovskiy. The Soviets frequently painted battle slogans on their tanks, as well as the names of famous Soviet citizens or soldiers, or the names of communities that had donated funds for the purchase of war equipment.

**77.** A Soviet T-34-85 tank unit prepares for action in the early phase of the Berlin offensive in May 1945. During the Berlin fighting, some 1,500 German armoured vehicles faced 6,250 Soviet tanks and assault guns. (Sovfoto)

76▲   77▼

▲ 78

78. A pair of T-34 Model 1943 in the streets of Berlin in May 1945. Although the T-34 Model 43 had gone out of production in 1944, some were still in service until the very end of the war. The white turret band was an Allied recognition sign to prevent

Anglo-American fighter-bombers attacking Soviet armoured columns.

79. A pair of T-34-85 on one of Berlin's bridges during the fighting there in May 1945. (Sovfoto)

80. A column of T-34-85 tanks proceed down a street in Berlin during the May 1945 battle. (Sovfoto)

81. Soviet tanks like this IS-2m to the left had screening added to the turret to ward off the

ubiquitous German Panzerfaust infantry anti-tank rockets. The screening detonated the warhead of the rocket at a safe distance from the main armour of the tank.

▼ 79

◀82
83▲

**82.** Another example of stand-off screening for protection against Panzerfausts, this time on a T-34-85 near the Brandenburg Gate. In this case, the screens were made by simply attaching bed springs to the tank.

**83.** An ISU-122 assault gun passes a sign vainly proclaiming that Berlin will remain German. (Sovfoto)

**84.** An IS-2m Stalin heavy tank stationed near the Brandenburg Gate at the conclusion of the fighting in Berlin in May 1945. The white turret identity band is evident in this view, as is the regimental insignia, a white bear on a red star. (Sovfoto)

84▼

▲85   ▼86

**85.** IS-2m heavy tanks prowl the streets during the final days of the fighting in Berlin in 1945. These tanks belong to the same regiment as the tank in the preceding picture but seem to have the unit insignia and numbering absent.

**86.** There has always been some controversy over whether the IS-3 heavy tank actually saw combat during the Second World War. According to Soviet sources, this is a view of an IS-3 taking part in the fighting near Berlin in May 1945.

**87.** A BA-64B scout car takes part in a victory celebration near the Reichstag building in Berlin on 20 May 1945. The slogan on the bow of the BA-64B reads 'Glory to Stalin' and the slogan on the side says 'Caucasus–Berlin'.

## The *Fotofax* series

A new range of pictorial studies of military subjects for the modeller, historian and enthusiast. Each title features a carefully-selected set of photographs plus a data section of facts and figures on the topic covered. With line drawings and detailed captioning, every volume represents a succinct and valuable study of the subject. New and forthcoming titles:

**Warbirds**
F-111 Aardvark
P-47 Thunderbolt
B-52 Stratofortress
Stuka!
Jaguar
US Strategic Air Power:
  Europe 1942–1945
Dornier Bombers
RAF in Germany

**Vintage Aircraft**
German Naval Air Service
Sopwith Camel
Fleet Air Arm, 1920–1939
German Bombers of WWI

**Soldiers**
World War One: 1914
World War One: 1915
World War One: 1916
Union Forces of the American
  Civil War
Confederate Forces of the
  American Civil War
Luftwaffe Uniforms
British Battledress 1945–1967
  (2 vols)

**Warships**
Japanese Battleships, 1897–
  1945
Escort Carriers of World War
  Two
German Battleships, 1897–
  1945
Soviet Navy at War, 1941–1945
US Navy in World War Two,
  1943–1944
US Navy, 1946–1980 (2 vols)
British Submarines of World
  War One

**Military Vehicles**
The Chieftain Tank
Soviet Mechanized Firepower
  Today
British Armoured Cars since
  1945
NATO Armoured Fighting
  Vehicles
The Road to Berlin
NATO Support Vehicles

## The *Illustrated* series

The internationally successful range of photo albums devoted to current, recent and historic topics, compiled by leading authors and representing the best means of obtaining your own photo archive.

**Warbirds**
US Spyplanes
USAF Today
Strategic Bombers, 1945–1985
Air War over Germany
Mirage
US Naval and Marine Aircraft
  Today
USAAF in World War Two
B-17 Flying Fortress
Tornado
Junkers Bombers of World War
  Two
Argentine Air Forces in the
  Falklands Conflict
F-4 Phantom Vol II
Army Gunships in Vietnam
Soviet Air Power Today
F-105 Thunderchief
Fifty Classic Warbirds
Canberra and B-57
German Jets of World War Two

**Vintage Warbirds**
The Royal Flying Corps in
  World War One
German Army Air Service in
  World War One
RAF between the Wars
The Bristol Fighter
Fokker Fighters of World War
  One
Air War over Britain, 1914–
  1918
Nieuport Aircraft of World War
  One

**Tanks**
Israeli Tanks and Combat
  Vehicles
Operation Barbarossa
Afrika Korps
Self-Propelled Howitzers
British Army Combat Vehicles
  1945 to the Present
The Churchill Tank
US Mechanized Firepower
  Today
Hitler's Panzers
Panzer Armee Afrika
US Marine Tanks in World War
  Two

**Warships**
The Royal Navy in 1980s
The US Navy Today
NATO Navies of the 1980s
British Destroyers in World
  War Two
Nuclear Powered Submarines
Soviet Navy Today
British Destroyers in World
  War One
The World's Aircraft Carriers,
  1914–1945
The Russian Convoys, 1941–
  1945
The US Navy in World War
  Two
British Submarines in World
  War Two
British Cruisers in World War
  One
U-Boats of World War Two
Malta Convoys, 1940–1943

**Uniforms**
US Special Forces of World
  War Two
US Special Forces 1945 to the
  Present
The British Army in Northern
  Ireland
Israeli Defence Forces, 1948 to
  the Present
British Special Forces, 1945 to
  Present
US Army Uniforms Europe,
  1944–1945
The French Foreign Legion
Modern American Soldier
Israeli Elite Units
US Airborne Forces of World
  War Two
The Boer War
The Commandos World War
  Two to the Present
Victorian Colonial Wars

A catalogue listing these series and other Arms & Armour Press titles is available on request from: Sales Department, Arms & Armour Press, Artillery House, Artillery Row, London SW1P 1RT.